Emergency 999!

Stories by Jane Langford
and Tony Ashton

Illustrated by David Kearney

CONTENTS

Bee Attack! 3
by Jane Langford

Tractor Terror! 13
by Tony Ashton

Flood Rescue 24
by Tony Ashton

Bee Attack!

Bee stings can be painful.
But if you are allergic to them, they can also be very dangerous.
Kim was allergic to bee stings.
She had to have her medicine with her all the time. On the day of the school trip she really needed it.

It was the end of the day. Everyone was waiting for the coach and everyone was tired. Kim sat on the grass with her friend, Jay.

"Let's roll down the hill," said Jay. "I bet I get to the bottom first."

"OK," said Kim. "Let's go!"

Kim and Jay rolled down the hill.
At the bottom of the hill was a
big bush. Kim rolled into it.
Then she heard a loud buzzing noise.
"Oh no!" cried Kim. "Bees!"
Kim had rolled right into a bees' nest.

Bees flew up around Kim in a big black cloud. She was very frightened.
"Help!" she screamed. "Help!"
Mrs Patel turned round.
She saw the bees buzzing round Kim.
"Oh no!" she cried. "Kim is allergic to bee stings!"

Mrs Patel ran down the hill.
She pulled Kim out of the bush.
Kim was covered in big red lumps.
The bees had stung her lots of times.

Just then the coach arrived.
The coach driver saw the angry
bees buzzing around Kim.
He told the rest of the children to
get onto the coach.
They could hear Kim screaming.
Suddenly Kim stopped screaming.
She went very white and began to
gasp for breath.

"Help me get Kim onto the coach," said Mrs Patel.

The coach driver carried Kim onto the coach. Some of the bees followed them and the children started to scream.

"Be quiet!" shouted Mrs Patel. "Kim is very sick! She needs her medicine or she will die!"

The children stopped screaming.
They shut the door to keep out the
rest of the bees.

"Where is Kim's medicine bag?"
asked Mrs Patel.

"I'll look for it," said Jay.
But he couldn't find it.

"It's not here," he said. "Kim must have left it back at school."

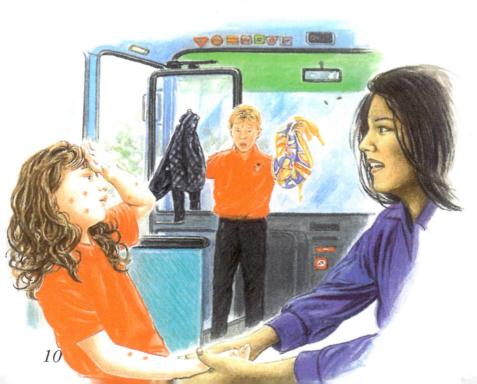

This was terrible!

Kim needed her medicine.

If she did not have an injection she would die.

"I'll call for an ambulance!" said the coach driver.

"Hurry up!" said Mrs Patel. "Kim could be dead in twenty minutes!"

Everyone was very frightened.

They didn't want Kim to die.

Suddenly Jay shouted, "Look, the ambulance is here!"
The ambulance men gave Kim an injection. They were just in time to save her life. Kim was very lucky. She never forgot her medicine bag again!

Tractor Terror!

Many people go on holiday in the country. They like the peace and quiet. But the country can be a dangerous place. As Shane found out.

Shane lived with his mum and dad in the town. One summer he went for a holiday on a farm with his gran and grandad. Shane liked it on the farm. He liked helping Mr Jones, the farmer. He helped him to milk the cows and feed the hens. Best of all he liked to watch Mr Jones driving the tractor.

"You are like Mr Jones' shadow!"
said Grandad.
"What do you mean?" asked Shane.
"You go everywhere that he goes,"
said Gran, "just like a shadow."
"I like my new shadow!" said Mr Jones.

One morning Shane woke up early.
His gran and grandad were still asleep.
I'll go and find Mr Jones,
thought Shane.
Shane looked everywhere.
But he couldn't find Mr Jones.

Shane looked across the big field.
He could hear the tractor.
But he could not see it.
The tractor was making a funny noise.
Shane wondered what Mr Jones was doing. He set off across the field to find out.

Soon Shane could see the tractor. It had fallen over and Mr Jones was trapped. The blades of the cutter were still turning.

They were right by Mr Jones' head and they were getting closer.

Mr Jones looked very pale and he had a cut on his head.

"Shane," he said, "thank goodness you're here. You must pull the lever to stop the blades turning – before they cut me."

Shane climbed inside the tractor.
But there were *two* levers!
He knew that one lever would
stop the blades turning.
But what would the other lever do?

He didn't know which lever to pull.
But he had to choose one.
Bravely, Shane pulled one of
the levers…

The blades stopped turning.
Then Shane turned off the engine.
"Well done, Shane," said Mr Jones.
"Now run back to the house and dial 999."

The fire brigade helped Mr Jones to get out from under the tractor.
"Thanks, Shane," said Mr Jones. "You saved my life. I might have died if you hadn't followed me."
"That's OK," said Shane. "I like being your shadow!"

FLOOD RESCUE

It always rains in the winter, but one winter the rain never seemed to stop. The rivers were full and many roads were flooded. One family got caught in a flood…

It had rained all day.
Dad had promised to take Holly and Josh to the cinema.
"We are still going to the cinema, aren't we?" asked Holly.
"Well, it's not a nice night for driving," said Dad.
"Oh, go on Dad," said Josh.

So Dad, Holly and Josh ran to the car and climbed in.
Dad drove slowly along the road.
"Look how high the river is!" said Holly.
"It's nearly up to the road," said Josh.

Dad drove round a corner. He did not know there was a dip in the road.
The dip was full of water.
The car went into the water and Dad slammed on the brakes.
Then the car swung round.
Dad turned the steering wheel.
The car slid from side to side and stopped. Then the engine cut out.

Dad tried to start the car but the engine was dead. Josh wiped the window with his hand and looked out. The river was rising and water was rushing down into the dip.
"I want to go home!" said Josh.

Dad tried to open the car door but there was too much water.
He couldn't push the door open.
"Look, there's water coming up from the floor!" cried Holly.
"We're all going to drown!" shouted Josh.

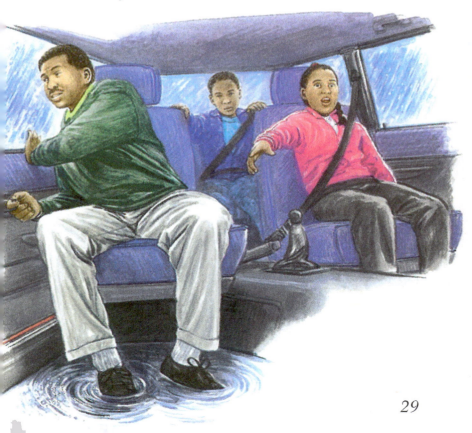

"It's OK, Josh," said Dad. "I'll dial 999 on my mobile phone."

"They will get here in time won't they, Dad?" asked Holly.

"Of course they will," said Dad.

But he was not so sure.

"How will they get to us?" asked Josh. "The water is getting deeper!"

"Don't worry, Josh," said Dad. "They'll think of something."

Soon Holly heard a noise.
It was a rescue helicopter.
A man on a rope shouted down to them, "Climb out of the windows and get onto the car roof."
Dad, Josh and Holly climbed out of the car. It wasn't easy.
Then the rescue helicopter lifted them to safety.

"You've had a very lucky escape," said the rescue man. "The river has flooded and some cars have been washed away."
Dad looked at Holly and Josh.
He knew they were lucky to be alive.